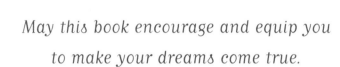

To _____

May this book encourage and equip you
to make your dreams come true.

From _____

Date _____

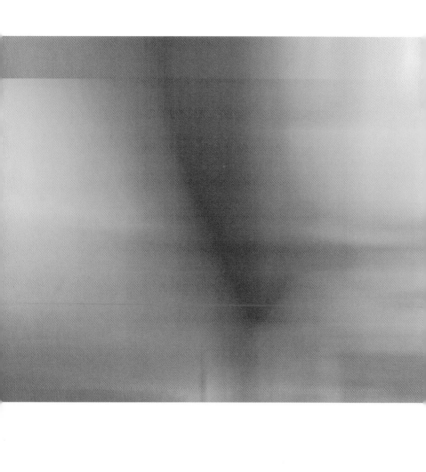

John C. Maxwell

DARE TO DREAM
...... THEN DO IT

WHAT SUCCESSFUL PEOPLE KNOW AND DO

COUNTRYMAN

NASHVILLE, TENNESSEE

Published in association with Yates & Yates, LLP, Attorneys and Counselors, Orange, California

Design: The DesignWorks Group; cover, Wes Youssi; interior, Robin Black
        www.thedesignworksgroup.com

ISBN 1 4041 0188 8

Printed and bound in the United States of America

www.thomasnelson.com | www.jcountryman.com

www.injoy.com

contents

Introduction

Everybody has a dream deep down inside. What's yours? Is it to climb the world's highest mountains? To build a world–class business? To become a senator or even president? To raise a healthy family? To win championships? To fly? If you could do *anything*, what would it be?

Most people don't achieve great dreams. They give up. They fall short. They get off track. They settle. Or they dream too small!

When I was in college and imagined my career, my lifetime goals were so small that I achieved them in my second position—within five years of graduating. That's when I decided to stop setting goals and start dreaming.

Theologian Frederick Henry Hedge said, "Dreaming is an act of pure imagination, attesting in all men a creative power, which if it were available in waking, would make every man a Dante or a Shakespeare." You have the potential to be a Shakespeare or an Edison or a Churchill or a Curie or a King. Only two things stand in your way: dreaming it . . . and then doing it.

Have you dared to dream, I mean *really* dream? If something is within your apparent reach, it isn't a dream. If you wouldn't have to stretch beyond what you think is possible, then it isn't a dream. Bold dreams change you as they change the world around you.

MAYBE YOU'RE AFRAID OF A BIG DREAM. You don't want to fail. Nobody does. But safe living leads to regret later on in life. U.S. President Theodore Roosevelt said:

> Far better it is to dare mighty things, to win glorious triumphs, even though checkered by failure, than to rank with those poor spirits who neither enjoy much nor suffer much, because they live in the gray twilight that knows neither victory nor defeat.

Someone once said, "Don't let yourself be pressured into thinking that your dreams or your talents aren't prudent. They were never meant to be prudent. They were meant to bring joy and fulfillment to your life."

What's the *worst* thing that could happen if you pursue your dream and don't achieve it? You could be where you are now. What's the *best* thing that could happen if you pursue your dream and don't achieve it? You could find yourself in new territory on the threshold of a *new* dream.

MAYBE YOU'RE LISTENING TO CRITICAL PEOPLE. Some people don't like to see others pursuing their dreams. The biblical story of Joseph, son of Jacob, is a classic example. Joseph dreamed big dreams. And what was the response of his brothers? They said, "Look, this dreamer is coming! Come therefore, let us now kill him" (Genesis 37:19, 20). People who aren't pursuing their own dreams are likely to criticize people who are.

MAYBE YOU DON'T KNOW HOW TO PURSUE YOUR DREAM. Successful people know and do things differently than unsuccessful people. That is a fact. If you have experienced a measure of success, you know this to be true. It starts with the way you think and dream, and it continues with how you live.

That is where I desire to help you. I have studied successful people my entire life. I have spent time with them. I have learned from them. What I have learned, I want to share with you. I want you to dare to dream, but I also want you to do more than that. I want you to do it: achieve your dream. I've written this book to help you do exactly that.

COMMIT TO
YOUR TRUE DREAM

Find out what you want
and go after it
as if your life depends on it.
Why? Because it does!
LES BROWN, BUSINESS CONSULTANT

If there were dreams to sell,
what would you buy?

THOMAS LOVELL BEDDOES, ENGLISH POET

Living and dreaming are
two different things—but you can't do
one without the other.

MALCOLM FORBES, MAGAZINE PUBLISHER

Hold fast to dreams,
for if dreams die,
life is a broken-winged bird
that cannot fly.

LANGSTON HUGHES, U.S. WRITER

A DREAM IS AN IDEAL involving a sense of possibilities rather than probabilities, of potential rather than limits. A dream is the **WELLSPRING OF PASSION**, giving us direction and pointing us to lofty heights. It is an **EXPRESSION OF OPTIMISM, HOPE, AND VALUES** lofty enough to capture the imagination and engage the spirit. **DREAMS GRAB US AND MOVE US.** They are capable of lifting us to new heights and overcoming self–imposed limitations.

ROBERT KRIEGEL, BUSINESS CONSULTANT

Music Dreams

If you're a music lover, you are probably familiar with the sounds of the classical guitar. What you might not know is that early in the twentieth century that style of music was largely developed by one individual. His name was Andres Segovia.

Born in southern Spain, Segovia began playing guitar as a small child. In those days the guitar was seen as little more than a folk instrument. It was not respected by serious composers and musicians the way orchestral instruments were. But Segovia saw great potential in the guitar for classical music.

Segovia began studying the techniques of classical musicians who played stringed instruments such as the violin and cello. He applied those techniques to his playing and developed other methods on his own. He adapted classical compositions of masters such as Bach and learned to play them on his instrument.

In 1909, Segovia made his classical debut—at the age of sixteen. In 1919, he toured the world and won over the classical establishment. Soon, for the first time, composers were writing classical music for guitar, and a whole new kind of music was born for the concert hall. Over the course of nearly eight decades, Segovia completely changed people's perception of his instrument.

But like many big dreams that become realized, Segovia's dream made an impact far beyond what he imagined. It could be argued that his efforts opened the door for the guitar, not only to the concert hall, but also to the jazz band. That in turn led to the electrically amplified guitar and rock music. If you've enjoyed the music of Les Paul or Chuck Berry or Jimi Hendrix or the Beatles or Van Halen or Green Day, then thank Andres Segovia. If it weren't for him and his dream, the music of the twentieth century would have gone in an entirely different direction.

When people discover their dreams and commit to them, there's no telling what kind of impact they will make.

Keep your eyes on the stars,
but remember to keep
your feet on the ground.

THEODORE ROOSEVELT, U.S. PRESIDENT

Happy are those who dream dreams
and are ready to pay the price
to make them come true.

CARDINAL LEON J. SUENENS

Don't let someone else create your world,
for when they do
they will always create it too small.

EDWIN LOUIS COLE, FOUNDER OF CHRISTIAN MEN'S NETWORK

Never measure the height of a mountain
until you have reached the top. Then you
will see how low it was.

The mightiest works have been accomplished
by men who have kept their ability to
dream great dreams.

What Kind of Dream Is It?

Daring dreams can be great things. Daring dreams have changed the world. Galileo had daring dreams to see the planets and developed the first telescope. Lindbergh had a daring dream and flew solo across the Atlantic Ocean. Ford had a daring dream. So did Ray Kroc. So did John F. Kennedy and Martin Luther King, Jr. Daring dreams change the world.

> What the mind can conceive and believe, it can achieve.

But there's a difference between a daring dream and a mere daydream. One fires you up and moves you forward. The other is nothing more than wishful thinking. Daring dreams are hills worth dying on in order to take them. Daydreams do little more than make you want to nap.

Take a look at some of the differences between the two.

Daring Dream	Daydream
Relies on Discipline	Relies on Luck
Focuses on the Journey	Focuses on the Destination
Cultivates Healthy Discontent	Cultivates Unhealthy Expectations
Maximizes the Value of Hard Work	Minimizes the Value of Hard Work
Leads to Action	Leads to Excuses
Creates Momentum	Creates Inertia
Breeds Teamwork	Breeds Isolation
Initiates	Waits
Embraces Risk as Necessary	Avoids All Risks
Makes You Responsible	Makes Others Responsible

Think about your dream. Does it inspire you to work hard? Does it motivate you to take smart risks? Does it build you up? Will it benefit others around you? As you move closer to fulfilling it, will it bring you closer to who you were born to be? Those are all hallmarks of a healthy daring dream!

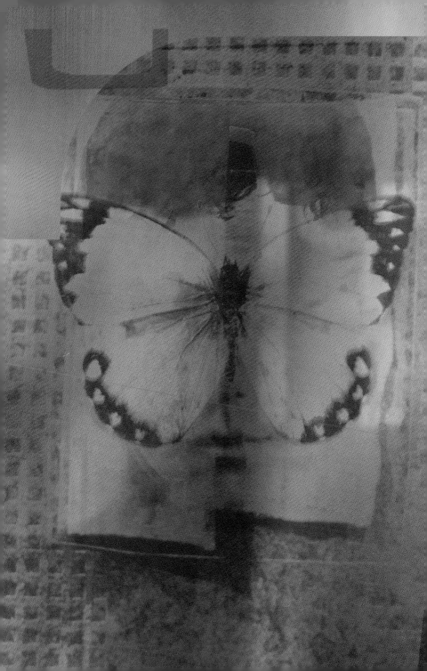

BELIEVE IN YOURSELF

Self-confidence is the
first requisite to great undertakings.

SAMUEL JOHNSON, ENGLISH AUTHOR & LEXICOGRAPHER

Something to Think About

What do you think of yourself? Do you believe in yourself? Are you confident? Les Brown knows the power of personal confidence. He is a successful person who communicates to employees of Fortune 500 companies and conducts seminars around the country. But life started out tough for him. He was born into extreme poverty and adopted by a single mother who lovingly raised him. Although he was identified as having a learning disability, his mother's love changed his life. He developed intellectually and socially, and he eventually served two terms in the Ohio state legislature.

In his book *Live Your Dreams,* Brown suggests four questions to ask to boost self–approval.

1. What are your gifts? What do you do well? If you have good health, acknowledge it. Be thankful if your family and your friends love you.
2. What are five things you like about yourself? You could include your appearance and/or qualities such as punctuality, honesty, and a loving spirit.

3. What people make you feel special? These individuals inspire something within you. What is it?
4. What moment of personal triumph do you remember? Take a moment to recall it.

Too many people dwell on the negative things about themselves instead of the positive. In one of his letters, Paul the apostle wrote:

> "Whatever things are true, whatever things are noble, whatever things are just, whatever things are pure, whatever things are lovely, whatever things are of good report, if there is any virtue and if there is anything praiseworthy—meditate on these things."
>
> PHILIPPIANS 4:8

That admonition applies to things about yourself as well as about the things of God. Think about all the things you have going for you. It will make a difference in how you look at yourself.

Self-trust is the essence of heroism.
RALPH WALDO EMERSON, ESSAYIST & POET

I tell people:
If you don't want to get into
positive thinking, that's okay.
Just eliminate all the negative thoughts
from your mind, and whatever's
left will be fine.
BOB ROTELLA, SPORTS PSYCHOLOGY SPECIALIST

AN OPTIMIST AND A PESSIMIST combined their resources and went into business together. Sales were fantastic, and after the first three months the optimist was elated.

"What a great beginning. Customers love our products, and we're selling more every week."

"Sure," replied the pessimist, "but if things keep going like this, we'll have to order more inventory."

Always be positive.
Think success,
not failure.

Fields are won by
those who believe in winning.
T. W. HIGGINSON, ABOLITIONIST & WOMEN'S RIGHTS ADVOCATE

Stick with the optimists.
It's going to be tough
even if they're right.
JAMES RESTON, SCOTTISH JOURNALIST

Confidence imparts a
wondrous inspiration to its possessor.
It bears him on in security,
either to meet no danger,
or to find matter of glorious trial.
JOHN MILTON, ENGLISH POET

Positively Possible

JOHN DOONER, chairman and chief executive of McCann–Erickson WorldGroup, helped build that company into the world's largest international ad agency, vaulting its gross income 70 percent from $1 billion in 1994 to $1.7 billion in 1997.

Dooner says the key is surrounding himself with positive people. Negative people, he says, aren't effective dreamers, and as such, they don't achieve great heights.

"It's only those people who believe in the dream and have the passion to make the dream come true that you want, because that's what makes it work and gets the job done faster," he said.

When he took over the helm at McCann–Erickson, he fired many staffers who didn't buy into his dream of creating the best agency possible. He wasn't going to let people with bad attitudes hold back the company. He knew that for dreams to come true, people must believe.

Early in life, I decided that
I would not be overcome by events.
My philosophy has been that
regardless of the circumstances,
I shall not be vanquished,
but will try to be happy.
Life is not easy for any of us.
But it is a continual challenge,
and it is up to us to be cheerful—
and to be strong, so that
those who depend on us
may draw strength from our example.

ROSE KENNEDY, KENNEDY FAMILY MATRIARCH

Don't Build a Monument
to Your Mistakes

ARNOLD PALMER is one of the great sportsmen of the twentieth century, and he really put professional golf on the map. Rick Reilly in *Sports Illustrated* said, "Basically, he took a game that was a little too prissy, a little too clubby, a little too saturated with Ivy League men trying not to soil their cardigans, and breathed sweet life into it." Or as Vin Scully said, "In a sport that was high society, he made it *High Noon.*"

> Good golfers don't dwell on bad performances—not if they want to remain good golfers.

Many people of my generation became golfers because of Arnold Palmer, just as the popularity of the game today has increased because of Tiger Woods. Palmer was a consummate golf professional. Like Woods, he started playing as a small boy. As he grew up, he performed just about every job he could on a golf course. (His father was a golf pro and course superintendent.)

Palmer has won ninety–two championships, sixty–two of them on the U.S. PGA tour. From 1960 to 1963, he was the greatest golfer in the world, winning twenty–nine PGA victories. That ability got him named *Sports Illustrated*'s Sportsman of the Year in 1960 and Athlete of the Decade according to an Associated Press poll. One writer said of Palmer that he combined "the boldness of a Brinks bandit with the fearless confidence of a man on a flying trapeze. He doesn't play a golf course, he assaults it."[i] And golf legend Bobby Jones once said, "If I ever had an eight–foot putt, and everything I owned depended on it, I'd want Arnold Palmer to take it for me."

EVEN THE BEST STUMBLE

One of the challenging things about golf is that anyone can have a really bad hole—even a hall–of–famer like Arnold Palmer. The key to playing through it is to forget about your bad shots. That can be a difficult thing to do—especially when someone erects a bronze monument to your mistake. That's what happened to Arnold Palmer.

It occurred at the 1961 Los Angeles Open at the peak of Palmer's career. On the par five ninth hole, his last of the day, Palmer hit a good drive and wanted to try to put the ball on the green with his second shot. That would put him in good position to attempt a birdie, putting him one stroke closer to the leaders.

With his three wood, Palmer hit what he believed was a good shot. But as the ball sailed, it faded to the right, hit a pole, and bounced out of bounds onto the driving range. Palmer dropped a ball, took a penalty stroke, and tried again. This time, his ball hooked to the left, and flew off the course into a road. Again he dropped a ball and took a penalty stroke. He repeated this process, hitting the ball out of bounds several times. Finally, he put the ball on the green. By then, he had accumulated ten strokes. It took him two more strokes with his putter to hole the ball. He finished with a twelve. And because of that, he went from a few strokes behind the leaders to being out of the tournament.

A MONUMENT TO FAILURE?

Today if you go to the ninth hole at the Rancho Park
Golf Course in Los Angeles, you will find a bronze
plaque that states: "On Friday, Jan. 6, 1961, the first
day of the 35th Los Angeles Open, Arnold Palmer,
voted Golfer of the Year and Pro Athlete of the Year,
took a 12 on this hole."

Good golfers don't dwell on bad performances—
not if they want to remain good golfers. And that has
always been true of Arnold Palmer. Once when asked
about his performance at the Open on hole nine, he
commented, "That doggone plaque will be there long
after I'm gone. But you have to put things like that
behind you. That's one of the wonderful things about
golf. Your next shot can be as good or bad as your last
one—but you'll always get another chance."ii

FROM *Failing Forward*

They can conquer
who believe they can.

JOHN DRYDEN, BRITISH POET AND PLAYWRIGHT

True prosperity is the
result of well-placed confidence in
ourselves and our fellow man.

BENJAMIN BURT, SILVERSMITH

Life is not easy for any of us.
But what of that? We must have perseverance
and, above all, confidence in ourselves.
We must believe that we are
gifted for something, and that this thing,
at whatever cost, must be attained.

MARIE CURIE, WINNER OF NOBEL PRIZES IN PHYSICS & CHEMISTRY

THINK DIFFERENTLY

Beware when the great God
lets loose a thinker on this planet.

RALPH WALDO EMERSON, ESSAYIST & POET

D. W. MacKinnon, a psychology professor, did research on creativity at the University of California at Berkeley in the 1970s. His tests showed that highly creative people were no different in intelligence from their less–creative colleagues, but they took longer to study problems and "played with" them more. So the difference was that the highly creative knew how to switch themselves into a playful mood. MacKinnon described this playful mood as being "more childlike."

Take Failure Out of the Equation

People who achieve their dreams usually experience a lot of failures along the way, but they don't let failure get the better of them. They get knocked down and get back up again. They think of themselves as achievers, as successes—even when things go wrong.

Here are six abilities that help successful people keep thinking right no matter how many obstacles they encounter:

1. SUCCESSFUL PEOPLE REJECT REJECTION. Author James Allen states, "A man is literally what he thinks, his character being the complete sum of all his thought." That's why it's important to make sure your thinking is on the right track.

   People who achieve their dreams don't give up trying because they don't base their self-worth on their performance. Instead, they have an internally based self-image. Rather than saying, "I am a failure," they say, "I missed that one" or "I made a mistake."

Psychologist Martin E. Seligman believes we have two choices when we fail: We can either internalize or externalize our failure. "People who blame themselves when they fail . . . think they are worthless, talentless, unlovable," says Seligman. "People who blame external events do not lose self–esteem when bad events strike." To keep the right perspective, take responsibility for your actions, but don't take failure personally.

2. SUCCESSFUL PEOPLE SEE FAILURE AS TEMPORARY. People who personalize failure see a problem as a hole they're permanently stuck in. But achievers see any predicament as temporary. For example, take the case of United States President Harry S. Truman. In 1922, he was thirty–eight years old, in debt, and out of work. In 1945, he was the most powerful leader of the free world. If he had seen failure as permanent, he would have remained stuck and never would have kept trying and believing in his potential. When successful people fail, they see it as a momentary event, not a life sentence.

3. **SUCCESSFUL PEOPLE SEE FAILURES AS ISOLATED INCIDENTS.** Author Leo Buscaglia once talked about his admiration for cooking expert Julia Child. He said: "I just love her attitude. She says, 'Tonight we're going to make a soufflé!' And she beats this and whisks that, and she drops things on the floor . . . and does all these wonderful human things. Then she takes the soufflé and throws it in the oven and talks to you for a while. Finally, she says, 'Now it's ready!' But when she opens the oven, the soufflé just falls flat as a pancake. But does she panic or burst into tears? No! She smiles and says, 'Well, you can't win them all. *Bon appétit!*'"

Achievers see every predicament as temporary.

4. **SUCCESSFUL PEOPLE SEE SUCCESS AS A PROCESS.** The greater the feat you desire to achieve, the greater the mental preparation required for

overcoming obstacles and persevering over the long haul. If you want to take a stroll in your neighborhood, you can reasonably expect to have few problems, if any. But that's not the case if you intend to climb Mount Everest.

It takes time, effort, and the ability to overcome setbacks. You have to approach each day with reasonable expectations and not get your feelings hurt when everything doesn't turn out perfectly.

Something that happened on baseball's opening day in 1954 illustrates the point well. The Milwaukee Braves and the Cincinnati Reds played one another, and a rookie for each team made their major-league debuts during that game. The rookie who played for the Reds hit four doubles and helped his team win with a score of 9–8. The rookie for the Braves went 0 for 5. The Reds player was Jim Greengrass, a name you may have never heard. The other guy, who didn't get a hit,

> Achievers are willing to vary their approaches to problems.

might be more familiar to you. His name was Hank Aaron, the player who became the best home–run hitter in the history of baseball.

If Aaron's expectations for that first game had been unrealistic, he might have given up baseball. Surely he wasn't happy about his performance that day, but he didn't think of himself as a failure. He had worked too hard for too long. He wasn't about to give up easily.

5. SUCCESSFUL PEOPLE ARE WILLING TO TRY A NEW APPROACH. In *The Psychology of Achievement,* Brian Tracy writes about four millionaires who made their fortunes by age thirty-five. They each were involved in an average of seventeen businesses before finding the one that took them to the top. They kept trying and changing until they found something that worked for them.

Achievers are willing to vary their approaches to problems. That's important in every walk of life, not just business. For example, if you're a fan of track and field events, you have undoubtedly enjoyed watching athletes compete in the high jump. I'm always amazed by the heights achieved by the men and women in those events. What's really interesting is that in the 1960s, the sport went through a major change in technique that allowed athletes to break the old records and push them up to new levels.

The person responsible for that change was Dick Fosbury. Where previous athletes used the straddle method to high jump, in which they went over the bar while facing it, with one arm and one leg leading, Fosbury developed a technique where he went over headfirst with his back to the bar. It was dubbed the Fosbury flop.

Developing a new high-jump technique was one thing. Getting it accepted by others was another matter. Fosbury remarked, "I was told over and over again that I would never be successful, that I was not going to be competitive and the technique was simply not going to work. All I could do was shrug and say, 'We'll just have to see.'"

And people did see. Fosbury won the gold medal in the Mexico City Olympics in 1968, shattering the previous Olympic record and setting a new world record in the process. Since then, nearly all world–class high jumpers use his technique. To achieve his dream, Fosbury had to try a new approach to high jumping.

6. SUCCESSFUL PEOPLE BOUNCE BACK. One thing all successes have in common is the ability to bounce back after an error, mistake, or failure. Psychologist Simone Caruthers says, "Life is a series of outcomes. Sometimes the outcome is what you want. Great. Figure out what you did right. Sometimes the outcome is what you don't want. Great. Figure out what you did [wrong] so you don't do it again." That's the key to bouncing back.

To achieve your dream, you cannot allow failure to stop you. You need to keep moving forward no matter what happens. And the ability to do that begins with your thinking. It is a battle of the mind. As General George S. Patton remarked, "If you are going to win any battle you have to do one thing. You have to make the mind run the body. Never let the body tell the mind what to do. The body will always give up." People who dare to dream—and then do it—don't give up.

ADAPTED FROM *Failing Forward*

If you have trouble
thinking outside of the box,
then blow up the box.

I make beanstalks;
I'm a builder, like yourself.

EDNA ST. VINCENT MILLAY, U.S. POET

A minute of thought
is worth more
than an hour of talk.

Change Your Mind

If you want to think differently from others so that you can achieve your dream, then heed the following advice:

1. GIVE YOURSELF THE TIME TO THINK. Most people keep themselves much too busy. They confuse activity with accomplishment. If you want to perform well, you need to think well. You can't do that if you never set aside time just for thinking.

2. FIND A PLACE TO BE CREATIVE. I believe that a person who possesses mental discipline can think anywhere. However, I also know that some environments are particularly conducive to creative thinking. I have a certain chair in my office that is my favorite place to think. Figure out what works for you.

3. FORCE YOURSELF TO THINK. If thinking were easy, everyone would be good at it—and everyone would be successful. The truth is that thinking can be hard work. That's why you need to make it a

discipline of your life. Give yourself a goal to think for a certain amount of time every day.

4. SEE PROBLEMS AS OPPORTUNITIES. People who achieve their dreams don't take no for an answer. They are undeterred by obstacles. And they see problems as opportunities. That, in a nutshell, is the essence of entrepreneurship: seeing opportunities in problems. Learn to think that way and you have unlimited resources for success.

5. CHALLENGE ASSUMPTIONS. One of the most insurmountable obstacles to successful thinking is the phrase, "But we've always done it this way." It was Robert Kriegel who said, "Sacred cows make the best burgers." You can't buy into the same assumptions as everyone else and think differently as successful people do. Don't take anything for granted.

6. EXPLORE EVERY OPTION. Unsuccessful people think there is one right answer to any problem. Successful people understand there are sometimes dozens. The

trick is to find as many as possible so you can use the *best* one for that given moment.

7. RECRUIT OTHER GOOD THINKERS TO HELP YOU. Nobody ever achieved a big dream alone. Successful people know that they are not big enough, smart enough, or strong enough to do everything themselves. They get help. If you want to succeed, work with others.

Real-Life Sherlock Holmes

Just about everyone has heard of Sherlock Holmes, the creation of British author Sir Arthur Conan Doyle. Holmes was inspired by one of Doyle's teachers, a man who had an eerie trick of spotting details. When Doyle, a physician by trade, decided to combine his love of both science and literature by writing mystery stories, he created a fictional detective who reduced the pursuit of criminals to "an exact science," modeled in part after his former teacher. That's how Sherlock Holmes was born.

What most people don't know is that Doyle used that same deductive ability in real life to free an innocent man from prison. George Edalji had been convicted and sentenced to seven years of hard labor for maiming horses, but Doyle reviewed the facts and punched holes in the prosecutor's case. The crimes had been committed at night, and the accused man was nearly blind. His eyesight would have made it impossible for him to climb over the hedges, rails, wires, and other obstacles to get to the stables. Based on Doyle's work, Edalji, an innocent man, was pardoned. And it happened because Doyle thought differently than others.

All things are filled full of signs,
and it is a wise man who can
learn about one thing from another.
PLOTINUS, ROMAN PHILOSOPHER

Thought is the original source
of all wealth, all success,
all material gain, all great discoveries
and inventions, and all achievement.
CLAUDE M. BRISTOL, U.S. AUTHOR

Take charge of your thoughts.
PLATO, GREEK PHILOSOPHER

How Do Successful People Think?

They think beyond themselves and their world to see
the *big picture.*

They remove distractions and mental clutter to
remain *focused.*

They break outside of their box and explore
options *creatively.*

They build a foundation on facts to see things *realistically.*

They create plans that will help them act *strategically.*

They find solutions in every situation by looking at
them *positively.*

They consider the past and gain perspective by
being *reflective.*

They reject the routine and don't accept it just because
it is *popular.*

They reach out to others to join them and think with
them *collaboratively.*

They consider others and add value to them *unselfishly.*

They focus on results knowing that the return comes
from the *bottom line.*

INSPIRED BY *Thinking for a Change*

TAKE ACTION

Dreams don't work
unless you do.

JOHN C. MAXWELL

If you have built castles in the air,
your work need not be lost;
there is where they should be.
Now put foundations under them.

HENRY DAVID THOREAU, ESSAYIST

It is only our deeds
that reveal who we are.

CARL G. JUNG, PSYCHIATRIST

Wouldn't Take No for an Answer

In 1947, LESTER WUNDERMAN was arbitrarily fired from his advertising job in New York. But the young man felt he still had a lot to learn from the head of the agency, Max Sackheim. So the next morning, Wunderman went back to his office and began working just as he had before. He talked to coworkers and clients; he sat in on meetings—all without pay.

Sackheim ignored him for a month.

When the month was over, the temperamental Sackheim walked up to Wunderman. "Okay, you win," he said, shaking his head. "I never saw a man who wanted a job more than he wanted money."

> Goals are nothing without action.

That kind of persistence and an inclination toward action paid off for Wunderman. He went on to be one of the most successful advertising men of the century and is known as the father of direct marketing. He is credited with having invented preprinted newspaper inserts, bound–in subscription cards for magazines, and subscription clubs such as those used by Time–Life Books and the Columbia Record Club.

Advertising may not be your thing, but action must be. What are you willing to do to achieve your dream? What are you willing to do *even if you must do so for free?* Success begins by beginning. And it continues with consistent action.

Anytime I want to make a change
or achieve anything in my life,
I write it down, along with
my plan to accomplish the goal
and when I will achieve it.
In this way, I turn
each of my goals into action.
SHAD HELMSTETTER, BEHAVIORAL RESEARCHER

Action Thoughts

1. You don't have to be great to start, but you have to start to be great.

2. The first two letters in the word *goal* are G–O.

3. Some people dream of worthy accomplishments while others wake up and do them.

4. Anybody who brags about what he is going to do tomorrow probably did the same thing yesterday.

5. People will never be what they ought to be until they are doing what they ought to be doing.

The time is always right
to do what is right.

MARTIN LUTHER KING, JR., CIVIL RIGHTS LEADER

I do not believe in a fate
that falls on men however they act;
but I do believe in a fate
that falls on them unless they act.

G.K. CHESTERTON, ENGLISH AUTHOR

For as long as he coached,
Paul "Bear" Bryant had this sign hanging
in his locker room:
"Cause something to happen."

Just Another Step Forward

KEMMONS WILSON has always been an initiator. He started working when he was seven years old and hasn't stopped since. He began by selling magazines, newspapers, and popcorn. In 1930 at the ripe old age of seventeen, he decided to try working for someone else, and he made twelve dollars a week writing figures on the price board of a cotton broker.

When a bookkeeper's job at thirty–five dollars a week opened up, Wilson applied for it and got it. But when he received his pay, it was still only twelve dollars. He requested a raise, and got one. The next week he received an additional three dollars. When Wilson asked why he didn't get the same thirty–five dollars as the other bookkeeper, he was told the company wouldn't pay that kind of money to a

> Most people would have complained and then forgotten about it. But Wilson, always a person of action, decided to do something about it.

seventeen–year–old kid. Wilson gave his notice. That was the last time he worked for someone else in more than seventy–five years.

Wilson made money in a variety of businesses after that: pinball machines, soft drink distribution, and vending machines. And he was able to save enough money to build his mother a house. That's when he realized home building had a lot of potential. He went into the construction business in Memphis and made a fortune capitalizing on the post–war building boom.

Wilson's initiative made him a lot of money, but it didn't make an impact on the world—not until 1951, that is. That was the year the Memphis businessman took his family on vacation to Washington, D.C. On that trip, he learned about the sorry state of hotel lodging in the United States. Motels had sprung up all over the country since the 1920s. Some were nice family places. Others rented beds by the hour. The problem was a traveler didn't know which he would find.

"You never could tell what you were getting," Wilson recalled later. "Some of the places were too squalid for words. And they all charged for children. That made my Scottish blood boil." A guy like Wilson who had five children really took a beating. Motels charged four dollars to six dollars a night for a room, plus two dollars per child. It tripled his bill.

Most people would have complained and then forgotten about it. But Wilson, always a person of action, decided to do something about it. "Let's go home and start a chain of family hotels," he said to his wife, "hotels with a name you could trust." His goal was four hundred hotels. His wife just laughed.

When Wilson returned to Memphis, he hired a draftsman to help him design his first hotel. He wanted it to be clean, simple, and predictable. And he wanted it to have all the things he and his family had wanted, such as a television in every room and a pool at every inn.

It's just too hard for a person of action to stop making things happen.

The next year he opened his first hotel on the outskirts of Memphis. Out front on a sign fifty–three feet tall flashed its name: Holiday Inn.

It took Wilson longer than he expected to reach four hundred hotels. By 1959, he had one hundred. But when he decided to franchise them, that boosted the openings. By 1964, there were five hundred Holiday Inns. In 1968, there were one thousand. And by 1972, a Holiday Inn opened somewhere in the world every seventy–two hours. The chain was still growing in 1979 when Wilson stepped down from the company's leadership after a heart attack.

"I was so hungry when I was young," Wilson said, "I just had to do something to make a living. And when I retired after my heart attack, I went home to smell the roses. That lasted about a month." It's just too hard for a person of action to stop making things happen.

FROM *The 21 Indispensable Qualities of a Leader*

A good plan vigorously executed
right now is far better than
a perfect plan executed next week.

GEORGE S. PATTON, U.S. GENERAL

Whatever you can do,
or dream you can do, begin it.
Boldness has genius,
power, and magic in it.

AUTHOR UNKNOWN, OFTEN ATTRIBUTED TO
GERMAN POET JOHANN WOLFGANG VON GOETHE

At the Day of Judgment,
we shall not be asked
what we have read,
but what we have done.

THOMAS À KEMPIS, GERMAN MONK

DEVELOP GREAT PEOPLE SKILLS

The most important single ingredient
in the formula for success is
knowing how to get along with people.

THEODORE ROOSEVELT, U.S. PRESIDENT

No man is an island.

JOHN DONNE, ENGLISH AUTHOR

How far you go in life
depends on your being tender with the
young, compassionate with the aged,
sympathetic with the striving,
and tolerant of the weak and strong.
Because some day in life
you will have been all of these.

GEORGE WASHINGTON CARVER, AGRICULTURAL CHEMIST

Half of the harm that is done
in this world is due to people who
want to feel important.
They do not mean to do harm . . .
They are absorbed in the endless
struggle to think well of themselves.

T. S. ELIOT, ENGLISH AUTHOR

A Life-Changing Shift in Focus

I read an article about actress ANGELINA JOLIE who experienced a paradigm shift a few years ago when she read a script. Prior to that, Jolie, who won an Oscar in 1999 for her role in *Girl, Interrupted,* could have been the poster girl for a life adrift. The child of actors Jon Voight and Marcheline Bertrand, she had grown up in Hollywood and indulged in many of its excesses, and she was well known for outrageous behavior and sometimes self–destructive actions. She was convinced she would die young.

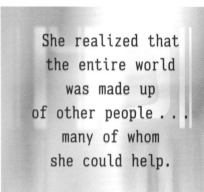

She realized that the entire world was made up of other people . . . many of whom she could help.

"There was a time where I never had a sense of purpose, never felt useful as a person," says Jolie. "I think a lot of people have that feeling—wanting to kill yourself or take drugs or numb yourself out because you can't shut it off or you just feel bad and you don't know what it's from."[iii]

Success in movies did little to help her. "I felt so off balance all the time," admits Jolie. "I remember one of the most upsetting times in my life was after I had attained success, financial stability and I was in love, and I thought, 'I have everything that they say you should have to be happy and I'm not happy.'"[iv]

> "If you've built schools or raised a child or done something to make things better . . . it just feels better."

But then she read the script for *Beyond Borders*, the story of a woman living a life of privilege who discovers the plight of refugees and orphans around the world. Jolie recalls, "Something in me really wanted to understand what the film was about, these people in the world, all these displaced people and war and famine and refugees."[v] For a year she traveled around the world with United Nations workers. "I got my greatest life education and changed drastically," she observes. She visited camps in Sierra Leone, Tanzania, Côte d'Ivoire, Cambodia, Pakistan, Namibia, and Thailand. Her entire perspective changed. She realized that the world was made up of other people, many of whom were in dire circumstances, many of whom she could help.

When the U.N. High Commissioner for Refugees asked her to become a goodwill ambassador in 2001, she was happy to do it. She also began donating money to help refugees and orphans, including three million dollars to the U.N. refugee program. (She says she makes a "stupid amount of money" to act in movies.)[vi] And she adopted a Cambodian orphan, Maddox. Recently *Worth* magazine listed her as one of the twenty–five most influential philanthropists in the world. She estimates that she gives almost a third of her income to charity.[vii]

Jolie puts it into perspective: "You could die tomorrow and you've done a few movies, won some awards—that doesn't mean anything. But if you've built schools or raised a child or done something to make things better for other people, then it just feels better. Life is better."[viii] Why does she feel that way? Because she finally gets the big picture. She stopped focusing on herself and began putting other people ahead of herself. And that is the first step when it comes to developing great people skills.

FROM *Winning With People*

When we understand the other fellow's
viewpoint . . . understand what
he is trying to do . . . nine times out
of ten he is trying to do right.

HARRY S TRUMAN, U.S. PRESIDENT

Relationships help us define
who we are and what we become.

DONALD CLIFTON AND PAULA NELSON

Keep a fair-sized cemetery
in your backyard, in which to bury the
faults of your friends.

HENRY WARD BEECHER, PASTOR & ABOLITIONIST

Unfair Question?

An experienced nurse is said to have recounted this story:

> During my second month of nursing school our professor gave us a pop quiz. I was a conscientious student and had breezed through the questions, until I read the last one: "What is the first name of the woman who cleans the school?" Surely this was some kind of joke! I had seen the cleaning woman several times. She was tall, dark–haired, and in her fifties, but how would I know her name? I handed in my paper, leaving the last question blank. Before class ended, one student asked if the last question would count toward our quiz grade. "Absolutely," said the professor. "In your careers you will meet many people. *All* are significant. They deserve your attention and care, even if all you do is smile and say hello." I've never forgotten that lesson. I also learned her name was Dorothy.

Who in your life have you simply walked by who deserved your attention? Don't let another day go by before pausing to connect with that individual.

No matter how much work you can do,
no matter how engaging your personality
may be, you will not advance far in business
if you cannot work through others.

JOHN CRAIG

He who has so little knowledge
of human nature as to seek happiness by
changing anything but his own
disposition will waste his life in
fruitless efforts and multiply the grief
which he purposes to remove.

SAMUEL JOHNSON, ENGLISH AUTHOR & LEXICOGRAPHER

We judge ourselves
by what we feel capable of doing,
while others judge us
by what we have already done.

HENRY WADSWORTH LONGFELLOW, U.S. POET

Five Things I Know About People

1. Everybody wants to be somebody.

2. Nobody cares how much you know until they know how much you care.

3. Everybody needs somebody.

4. Anybody who helps somebody influences lots of bodies.

5. Somebody today will rise up and become somebody.

If you're not comfortable with yourself,
you can't be comfortable with others.

SYDNEY J. HARRIS, JOURNALIST

It's Not About the Ship

During World War II, the Allies desperately needed warships. HENRY J. KAISER knew this, and as a shipbuilder, he wanted to find a way to increase his company's production. He knew the key to the problem wouldn't be found in improved engineering or upgraded materials. It was in understanding the people—the workers in the shipyards.

Kaiser knew people loved competition, so he told his employees in his Richmond, California, facility that he wanted to see whether they could break records. He didn't give them a specific goal, but he did tell them they were being timed. The builders in the yard worked faster and faster, each time trying to beat their previous records. And in the process, they volunteered more than two hundred fifty suggestions to increase production. One team built a ship in a remarkable four days, fifteen hours, twenty–six minutes. And his shipyard workers built Liberty ships in an astounding seventy–two days, while the national average was one hundred fifty!

Nothing is impossible when you understand how to communicate with people and lead them effectively.

Treat a man as he appears to be
and you make him worse.
But treat a man as if he already were
what he potentially could be,
and you make him what he should be.

JOHANN WOLFGANG VON GOETHE, GERMAN POET

Trust is like a bank account—
you have got to keep making deposits
if you want it to grow.
On occasion, things will go wrong,
and you will have to make a withdrawal.
Meanwhile, it is sitting
in the bank earning interest.

MIKE ABRASHOFF, U.S. NAVY COMMANDER

Kindness is a language the dumb can speak
and the deaf can hear and understand.

CHRISTIAN BOVEE, U.S. AUTHOR

EFFECTIVE LEADERS remember and act upon the fact that all work is done ultimately by people, with people, through people, and for people. Leaders function by creating alignment around tasks, inspiring and relating to people. LEADERSHIP IS HIGH TOUCH. It is grounded in the four chambers of leadership's heart: intimacy, integrity, passion, and competence.

ROGER STAUB II

STAY WITH YOUR STRENGTHS

Each man has to seek out
his own special aptitude for a higher life
in the midst of the humble and
inevitable reality of daily existence.
Than this, there can be no
nobler aim in life.

MAURICE MAETERLINCK, BELGIAN WRITER & NOBEL LAUREATE

A Rule of Thumb for Successful Work

Work where you're
STRONGEST **80** percent
of the time.

Work where you're
LEARNING **15** percent
of the time.

Work where you're
WEAKEST **5** percent
of the time.

Help Others by Being Your Best

Staying with your strengths is not a selfish act. Not only is it good for you but it also helps others if you are part of a team.

Just about everyone has experienced being on some kind of team where people had to take on roles that didn't suit them: an accountant forced to work with people all day, a basketball forward forced to play center, a guitarist filling in on keyboard, a teacher stuck doing paperwork, a spouse who hates the kitchen taking on the role of cook.

> People working in an area of weakness resent that their best is untapped.

What happens to a team when one or more of its members constantly play "out of position"? First, morale erodes because the team isn't playing up to its capability. Then people become resentful. The people working in an area of weakness resent that their best is untapped. And other people on the team who know that they could better fill a mismatched position on the team resent that their skills are being overlooked. Before long, people become unwilling to work as a team. Then everyone's confidence begins to erode. And the situation just keeps getting worse. The team stops progressing, and the competition takes advantage of the team's obvious weaknesses. As a result, the team never realizes its potential. When people aren't where they do things well, things don't turn out well.

Having the right people in the right places is essential to team building. Take a look at how a team's dynamic changes according to the placement of people:

The Wrong Person in the Wrong Place = Regression
The Wrong Person in the Right Place = Frustration
The Right Person in the Wrong Place = Confusion
The Right Person in the Right Place = Progression
The Right People in the Right Places = Multiplication

It doesn't matter what kind of team you're dealing with: the principles are the same. Advertising giant David Ogilvy was right when he said, "A well–run restaurant is like a winning baseball team. It makes the most of every crew member's talent and takes advantage of every split–second opportunity to speed up service."

Right now you may not be sure what your greatest strengths are. If that is true, then follow these guidelines:

1. BE SECURE: My friend Wayne Schmidt says, "No amount of personal competency compensates for personal insecurity." If you allow your insecurities to get the better of you, you'll be inflexible and reluctant to change. And you cannot grow without change.

2. GET TO KNOW YOURSELF: You won't be able to find your niche if you don't know your strengths and weaknesses. Spend time reflecting and exploring your gifts. Ask others to give you feedback. Do what it takes to remove personal blind spots.

3. TRUST YOUR LEADER: A good leader will help you start moving in the right direction. If you don't trust your leader, look to another mentor for help. Or get on another team.

4. **SEE THE BIG PICTURE:** Your place on any team only makes sense in the context of the big picture. If your only motivation for finding your niche is personal gain, your poor motives may prevent you from discovering what you desire.

5. **RELY ON YOUR EXPERIENCE:** When it comes down to it, the only way to know that you've discovered your niche is to try what seems right and learn from your failures and successes.

When you discover what you were made for, your heart sings. It says, there's no place like this place anywhere near this place, so this must be the place!

FROM *The 17 Indisputable Laws of Teamwork*

He did each thing
as if he did nothing else.

SAID OF CHARLES DICKENS, AUTHOR UNKNOWN

Things which matter most
must never be at the mercy of
things which matter least.

JOHANN WOLFGANG VON GOETHE, GERMAN POET

First things first,
and last things not at all.

PETER DRUCKER, BUSINESS CONSULTANT

The real tragedy of life
is not in being limited to one talent,
but in the failure
to use the one talent.

EDGAR W. WORK

Make the Most of It

It's said that inventor THOMAS EDISON set himself an ambitious goal: to come up with a major new invention every six months and a minor one every ten days. When he died, he had 1,093 U.S. patents and more than two thousand foreign ones. He made his dreams reality by sticking with what he did best.

If a man has talent and cannot use it, he has failed. If he has a talent and uses only half of it, he has partly failed. If he has talent and learns somehow to use the whole of it, he has gloriously succeeded, and won a satisfaction and a triumph few men will ever know.

THOMAS WOLFE, U.S. NOVELIST

Start Where You Are

After striking out in a game, CHARLIE BROWN pours out his heart to Lucy: "I'll never be a big-league player! I just don't have it! All my life I've dreamed of playing in the big leagues, but I know I'll never make it!"

Lucy replies: "You're thinking too far ahead, Charlie Brown. What you need to do is set yourself more immediate goals. Start with the next inning, for example. When you go out to pitch, see if you can walk out to the mound . . . without falling down."

Genius is the gold in the mine;
talent is the miner
that works and brings it out.

LADY MARGUERITE BLESSINGTON, BRITISH AUTHOR

Imagine what a harmonious world
it could be if every single person,
both young and old, shared a little of
what he or she is good at doing.

QUINCY JONES, JAZZ MUSICIAN & ENTREPRENEUR

Well done, good and faithful servant;
you were faithful over a few things,
I will make you ruler over many things.
Enter into the joy of your lord.

JESUS CHRIST, IN MATTHEW 25:21

One Thing—and One Thing Only

"The musical output of five hundred years is summarized in BRAHMS' works," says biographer Karl Geiringer. "But these compositions are anything but servile imitations of preceding models. They are saved from this fate by the original personality of their master." And Johannes Brahms was one of *the* masters of music.

Music was everything to Brahms. He collected music and studied compositions going back to the fifteenth century. He worked feverishly to perfect his craft, refusing to publish anything that didn't meet his exacting standards. That is why he didn't publish his first symphony until he was forty years old. And he never married, saying that it would distract him from his vocation.

"I am in love with music," he once wrote. "I think of nothing but, and of other things only when they make music more beautiful for me."

Every man must at last
accept himself for his portion,
and learn to do his work
with the tools and talents
with which he has been endowed.
That some are more richly endowed than
others should cause no concern,
for in the final analysis it may appear
that the mighty oak is of less importance
than the tiny violet which blooms
in humble obscurity at its feet.

CHARLES A. HAWLEY

GET OUT OF
YOUR COMFORT ZONE

We forfeit three-fourths of ourselves
to be like other people.

ARTHUR SCHOPENHAUER, GERMAN PHILOSOPHER

Following the herd
is a sure way to mediocrity.

Investor's Business Daily

It is better by a noble boldness
to run the risk of being subject to
half the evils we anticipate
than to remain in cowardly listlessness
for fear of what may happen.

HERODOTUS, GREEK HISTORIAN

A successful leader has to be innovative.
If you're not one step ahead
of the crowd, you'll soon
be a step behind everyone else.

TOM LANDRY, NFL COACH

Characteristics of the Comfort Zone

We can't be out on the edge every second of every day. Everybody needs times to rest and become rejuvenated. However, if we stay in our comfort zones, we will never achieve anything of value. Our dreams lie out beyond the horizon. And just as ships were not built to stay in the harbor, we were not made to stay where it is safe. People are created to be resilient and resourceful.

Here are some good and bad things you need to know about the comfort zone:

1. In the comfort zone, MOST OF THE GAME IS PLAYED. Just as most of a football game is played in the middle of the field—between the twenty–yard lines—most of the game of life is played in the comfort zone. It's the place you must start before you try to make it to the end zone.

2. In the comfort zone, PEOPLE OFTEN LOSE INTEREST. What happens to people when nothing ever changes and they are never challenged? They get bored. Deep down, most people desire adventure.

But they will never experience it if they are unwilling to get out of their recliners.

3. In the comfort zone, MISTAKES ARE NOT AS COSTLY. One of the good things about the comfort zone is that the consequences of mistakes are not as dire. As you start to work toward your dreams, false starts and fumbles won't stop you permanently.

4. In the comfort zone, OPPOSITION IS NOT WELL FOCUSED. Another positive aspect of the comfort zone is that people are often relaxed there. That gives you an opportunity to get going. Only as you leave the comfort zone will the competition pick up.

5. In the comfort zone, VICTORY CANNOT BE ACHIEVED. If you are in the comfort zone and want to win, you must do what does not feel natural. You cannot stay comfortable and achieve victory. There is no guarantee that you will achieve it if you leave your comfort zone. But if you never leave your comfort zone, you are guaranteed *not* to achieve it.

Both fortune and love
befriend the bold.

OVID, ROMAN POET

Be brave enough to live creatively.
The creative is the place where no one
else has ever been. You have to leave the
city of your comfort and go into
the wilderness of your intuition.
You can't get there by bus, only by hard
work, risking, and by not quite knowing
what you're doing. What you'll discover
will be wonderful: yourself.

ALAN ALDA, ACTOR

God will help you be all you can be—
all you were originally designed to be.
But He will never permit you to be
successful at becoming someone else.

JOYCE MEYER, PASTOR

Not Waiting and Hoping for Success to Find Her

Just six months after founding her sportswear company in 1976, instead of sitting back and waiting for praise from the critics, designer LIZ CLAIBORNE ORTENBERG decided to get out of her comfort zone. She took off for a two–week trek through the malls of America. Her goal? To find out what shoppers liked—and didn't like—about her apparel. The company owner worked like a clerk and waited on customers in stores that carried her fashions. And she asked these customers dozens of questions.

She found out so much that it became a regular strategy she used to make her company successful.

"My goal was to gather as much information directly from the consumer as I could," says Claiborne. Her willingness to get out among the customers and learn from them paid off, too. In twenty-six years, she turned a small venture owned by her and two partners into a publicly held company with more than seven thousand employees worldwide and $3.7 billion in sales.

Ten Questions to Ask
Before Leaving Your Comfort Zone

1. Who else has done it?

2. How bad can it get?

3. How good can it get?

4. Can I first "try it on for size"?

5. Is there room for error?

6. Does the past say "yes"?

7. Is there enough momentum to make it?

8. Do I believe in myself?

9. Do I believe in my team?

10. How clearly has God spoken?

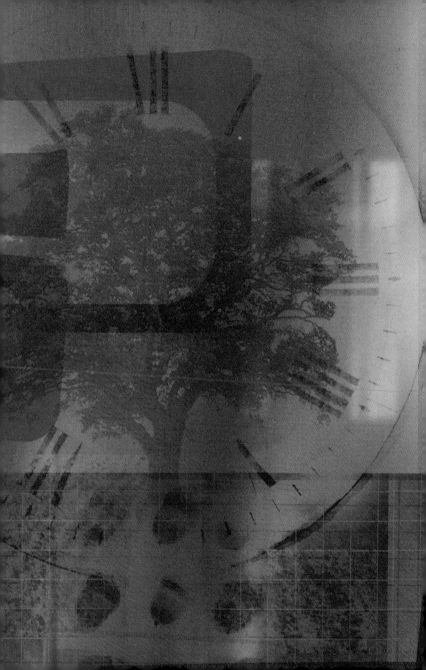

NEVER STOP LEARNING

They know enough
who know how to learn.

HENRY ADAMS, U.S. HISTORIAN

Learning and innovation go hand in hand.
The arrogance of success
is to think that what you did yesterday
will be sufficient for tomorrow.

WILLIAM POLLARD, BUSINESS LEADER

Learning is defined as a
change in behavior.
You haven't learned a thing
until you can
take action and use it.

DON SHULA AND KEN BLANCHARD

A time comes when you need to
stop waiting for the man
you want to become
and start being the man
you want to be.

BRUCE SPRINGSTEEN, MUSICIAN

The Ways We Learn

There are three classes of people in the world.

The first LEARN FROM THEIR OWN EXPERIENCE—
these are the WISE;

the second LEARN FROM THE EXPERIENCE OF OTHERS—
these are the HAPPY;

the third NEITHER LEARN FROM THEIR OWN
EXPERIENCE NOR THE EXPERIENCE OF OTHERS—
these are the FOOLS.

LORD CHESTERFIELD, ENGLISH STATESMAN

A Legacy of Learning and Change

Nokia is the largest producer of cellular phones in the world, but you'd probably never guess how the company got its start. It was formed over a century ago by FREDRIK IDESTAM. In the mid 1860s as the lumber industry in Finland started to boom, Idestam built a small pulp mill on the Emäkoski River and began making paper.

The first couple of years, the company struggled. But when Idestam won a bronze medal for his groundwood pulp at the 1867 Paris World's Fair, Nokia's sales took off, and it soon became firmly established. It excelled not only in its native Finland but explored and established markets in Denmark, Russia, Germany, England, and France. It wasn't long before the company had added two more paper facilities.

In the late 1890s, Nokia sought to diversify. The company built a water–driven electric power station near their first mill, and they attracted the Finnish Rubber Works as a customer. After a few years, the rubber company moved its operation to be near Nokia's power plant. Before long, the two companies became partners.

The companies did well during and after World War I. In 1922 they bought a controlling share of the Finnish Cable Works and did even better. They continued selling their existing products from the forestry and rubber industries, but the company's growth for the next forty years was driven by the sales that came from the cable works—from items such as power cables, telephone lines, and telephone equipment. By the 1960s, the company had four major business segments: forestry, rubber, cable, and electronics.

> Executives at Nokia knew that the company needed to change and improve or it would die.

During the next two decades, Nokia experienced some difficult times. A company focused on the past is not going to have a bright future. The 100–year–old company had become a huge conglomerate, and it was losing money. Executives at Nokia knew that the company needed to change and improve or it would die.

Solutions to organizational problems don't come from organizations; they come from the people, and that was the case at Nokia. In 1990, a young executive who had been with Nokia for five years was asked to take over the unprofitable mobile phones division of the company and turn it around. His name was JORMA OLLILA and his background was in finance and banking. He was so successful at the task that he was made the President and CEO of Nokia in 1992.

Ollila's next challenge was to turn the rest of the company around. His strategy was twofold. First, he determined to focus the organization's efforts in the area of greatest potential: communications technology. It was the next thing. That meant divesting the company of its other interests, including what had initially launched the company: rubber and paper. Second, Ollila wanted to replace trees with people, meaning that the company recognized that its value lay in human resources, not natural resources. That was especially important for a company whose business is technology. "The key challenge of technology companies today is how we renew ourselves," observes Ollila. "The technology cycles are shorter. We must build on our discontinuities and turn them into our favor."[ix]

Ollila is someone who personally knows the value of renewing himself. He has earned three master's degrees—in political science, economics, and engineering. He has taken the personal goal of self–improvement and made it a corporate one. The "Nokia Way" is grounded in four objectives: Customer Satisfaction, Respect for the Individual, Achievement, and Continuous Learning.

"Continuous Learning entitles everybody at Nokia to develop themselves and find ways to improve their performance," says Ollila. "And what's true for the individual is just as true for the company as a whole."[x]

> To improve an organization, you have to improve the individuals in that organization.

Ollila knows that to improve an organization, you have to improve the individuals in that organization. As a result, he has turned a money–losing conglomerate into a $20 billion global telecommunications enterprise. And Nokia continues to be an innovative leader in its field. Since 1992, the company has introduced dozens of significant market firsts. If your cell phone has a face plate with a special color or team logo, or it has different ring options, or it possesses a short–message chat function, you can thank the people at Nokia. They brought all those ideas to market. And they're still breaking new ground. Why? Because the people on the Nokia team are constantly learning and improving. As long as they keep getting better, so does Nokia.

"I don't think there is any other company which is better placed than we are to tackle the next paradigm," says Ollila. "This is an organization where, if you want to prove yourself, if you want to develop yourself, and grow yourself, we will give you the platform."[xi] They are always encouraging people to learn the next thing. By doing that, they all come closer to achieving their dreams.

FROM *The 17 Essential Qualities of a Team Player*

He who has no inclination to learn
more will be very apt
to think that he knows enough.

SIR JOHN POWELL, ENGLISH JUDGE

Some will never learn anything because
they understand everything too soon.

THOMAS BLOUNT, U.S. STATESMAN

The man who has ceased to learn
ought not to be allowed to wander around
loose in these dangerous days.

M. M. COADY, CANADIAN PRIEST & EDUCATOR

The Answer Is Not in the Stars

For centuries, ship captains wanted a way to determine their longitudinal positions while sailing. And for centuries great minds like those of Galileo and Newton looked to the stars for the answer. But the answer didn't lie there.

Instead the problem would be solved by an uneducated carpenter named JOHN HARRISON who knew the key to the problem was the creation of a reliable timepiece. That was no small problem in the 1700s. Shipboard clocks were notoriously inaccurate due to the sea's motion, atmospheric changes, and variations in temperature and humidity. But that didn't stop Harrison. He began working on the problem in the 1720s. He created clocks made of wood that produced their own grease. He developed metal alloys to produce pendulums that would work consistently in all kinds of weather. And then later he developed a clock that did away with the pendulum altogether.

All during the process, he met opposition from members of the British Parliament, which had offered twenty thousand pounds to whoever solved the problem.

But that didn't stop him. Over the course of more than thirty years, he developed four different clocks. And in the 1760s, he finally settled on one that he was satisfied would do the job. It was the first marine chronometer. And it forever changed ocean travel and the way we see the world.

Rules of the Learning Game

Leaders and learners alike need to derive meaning from events, to make projections from figures, to sculpt strategic plans from the chaos that often surrounds us.

1. Seize every opportunity to exchange knowledge.
2. Embrace contradiction.
3. Use brainstorming—it works.
4. Look at the big picture.

MARLENE CAROSELLI, LEADERSHIP CONSULTANT

CHAPTER
NINE

NEVER GIVE UP

"I can" is more important than "I.Q."
CLARK JOHNSON, BUSINESSMAN

If hard work is the key to success,
most people would rather pick the lock.

An enterprise,
when fairly once begun,
Should not be left
till all that ought is won.

I don't have anything against work.
I just figure, why deprive
somebody who really loves it.

When to Quit

A man goes to the Super Bowl, and when he arrives, he realizes that his seat is in the last row. After the game starts, he notices an empty seat right on the fifty–yard line. He makes his way to the empty seat and says to the man sitting next to it, "Excuse me, is anyone sitting here?" The man replies, "No, actually, the seat belongs to me. I was supposed to come with my wife, but she died. This is the first Super Bowl we haven't been at together since we got married in 1967."

"Well, that's terribly sad. But couldn't you find anyone else to take the seat? A close relative or friend?"

"No," the man replies. "They're all at the funeral."

Famous People's 90 Percent Sweat

It's said that success is 90 percent sweat and only 10 percent talent. Here are a few examples of the effort expended by "talented" people who succeeded:

CICERO practiced speaking before friends every day for thirty years to perfect his elocution.

PLATO wrote the first sentence of *The Republic* nine different ways before he was satisfied.

MILTON rose at four o'clock every morning to have enough hours for writing his *Paradise Lost*.

GIBBON spent twenty–six years on his *Decline and Fall of the Roman Empire*.

NOAH WEBSTER labored thirty–six years writing his dictionary, crossing the Atlantic twice to gather material.

BYRON rewrote one of his poetic masterpieces ninety–nine times before publication, and it became a classic.

Everything yields to diligence.

ANTIPHANES, GREEK PLAYWRIGHT

This is no time for ease and comfort.
It is time to dare and endure.

WINSTON CHURCHILL, ENGLISH STATESMAN

I have brought myself by long meditation
to the conviction that a human being
with a settled purpose must accomplish it,
and that nothing can resist
a will which will stake even existence
upon its fulfillment.

BENJAMIN DISRAELI, ENGLISH STATESMAN

They Never, Never, Never Quit

When WINSTON CHURCHILL received word that Hitler had invaded Russia, he contacted the BBC to schedule a broadcast from his weekend residence where he was staying. He was up most of the night working on his address. This is what he told the people of Britain:

> We have but one aim and one irrevocable purpose. We are resolved to destroy Hitler and every vestige of the Nazi regime. From this nothing will turn us—nothing. We will never parley. We will never negotiate with Hitler or any of his gang. We shall fight him by land. We shall fight him by sea. We shall fight him in the air, until with God's help we had rid the earth of his shadow and liberate its people from his yoke. Any man or state who marches with Hitler is our foe.

The tenacity of Churchill and the people of Britain kept the dream of freedom and democracy alive during Europe's darkest hours. They dared to dream— and then did it.

Badness you can get easily,
in quantity: the road is smooth,
and it lies close by.
But in front of excellence
the immortal gods have put sweat,
and long and steep is the way to it,
and rough at first.
But when you come to the top,
then it is easy,
even though it is hard.

HESIOD, GREEK POET

Great works are performed,
not by strength, but by perseverance.
He that shall walk, with vigor,
three hours a day, will pass,
in seven years, a space equal to the
circumference of the globe.

CHARLES JOHNSON

If you wish success in life,
make perseverance your bosom friend,
experience your wise counselor,
caution your elder brother
and hope your guardian genius.

JOSEPH ADDISON, ENGLISH WRITER, STATESMAN

Courage and perseverance have a magical
talisman before which difficulties
disappear and obstacles vanish into air.

JOHN QUINCY ADAMS, U.S. PRESIDENT

The Finisher

BOB IRELAND crossed the finish line on Thursday, November 6, 1986, as the New York City Marathon's 19,413th and final finisher—the first person to run a marathon with his arms instead of his legs. Bob was a forty–year–old Californian whose legs were blown off in Vietnam seventeen years before. In 1986, he recorded the slowest time in the Marathon's history: four days, two hours, forty-eight minutes, seventeen seconds.

When asked why he ran the race, he gave these three reasons: 1) to show he was a born–again Christian, 2) to test his conditioning, and 3) to promote physical fitness for others.

"Success is not based on where you start," said Ireland. "It's where you finish—and I finished."

DARE

The future belongs to those who believe
in the beauty of their dreams.
ELEANOR ROOSEVELT, U.S. FIRST LADY

So many of our dreams at first seem
impossible, then they seem improbable,
and then, when we summon the will,
they soon become inevitable.
CHRISTOPHER REEVE, ACTOR

A dream is the bearer of a new possibility,
the enlarged horizon, the great hope.
HOWARD THURMAN, MINISTER

TO DREAM . . .

We grow great by dreams.
All big men are dreamers.
They see things in the soft haze
of a spring day or in the red fire
of a long winter's evening.
Some of us let these dreams die,
but others nourish and protect them;
nurse them through bad days till they
bring them to the sunshine and light
which comes always to those who hope that
their dreams will come true.

WOODROW WILSON, U.S. PRESIDENT

. . . THEN

Whatever your hand finds to do,
do it with all your might.
ECCLESIASTES 9:10

All our dreams can come true,
if we have the courage to pursue them.
WALT DISNEY, ENTREPRENEUR

Don't be afraid of the space
between your dreams and reality.
If you can dream it, you can make it so.
BELVA DAVIS, BROADCAST JOURNALIST

Words without actions
are the assassins of idealism.
HERBERT HOOVER, U.S. PRESIDENT

DO IT!

Don't let what you can't do
interfere with what you can do.
AUTHOR UNKNOWN

I pray hard, work hard,
and leave the rest to God.
FLORENCE GRIFFITH JOYNER, OLYMPIC MEDALIST

Be both a speaker of words
and a doer of deeds.
HOMER, GREEK POET

Acknowledgements

Grateful acknowledgement is given to the following for permission to reprint material from the published works of John C. Maxwell:

The 17 Essential Qualities of the Team Player (Nashville: Thomas Nelson, Inc., 2002).

The 21 Indispensable Qualities of a Leader (Nashville: Thomas Nelson, Inc., 1999).

Falling Forward (Nashville: Thomas Nelson, Inc., 2000).

Winning with People (Nashville: Thomas Nelson, Inc., 2005).

i   Bert Randolf Sugar, *The 100 Greatest Athletes of All Time* (Secaucus, New Jersey: Citadel Press, 1995) p. 217.

ii   Allan Zullo with Chris Rodell, *When Bad Things Happen to Good Golfers: Pro Golf's Greatest Disasters* (Kansas City: Andrews McMeel Publishing, 1998) pp. 40–43.

iii   "Meet the New Angelina Jolie," www.cnn.com/2003/showbiz/movies/10/25/jolie.ap (accessed 13 January 2004).

iv   "Child Changes Everything," ABCNews.com, 17 October 2003.

v   Ibid.

vi   Ibid.

vii   Ibid.

viii   "Meet the New Angelina Jolie."

ix   Joyce Routson, "Nokia CEO Talks About Next–Generation Mobile Technology," <www.gsb.stanford.edu/news>, March 6, 2001.

x   "The Nokia Way," <www.nokia.com>, June 29, 2001.

xi   John S. McClenahen, "CEO of the Year," <www.industryweek.com>, November 30, 2000.

JOHN C. MAXWELL, known as America's expert on leadership, speaks in person to hundreds of thousands of people each year. He has communicated his leadership principles to Fortune 500 companies, the United States Military Academy at West Point, and sports organizations such as the NCAA, the NBA, and the NFL.

Maxwell is the founder of several organizations, including Maximum Impact, dedicated to helping people reach their leadership potential. He is the author of more than thirty books, including *The 360 Degree Leader, Developing the Leader Within You, Your Road Map for Success,* and *The 21 Irrefutable Laws of Leadership,* which has sold more than one million copies.

For more information about John Maxwell and his leadership resources, please visit:

www.injoy.com
or www.maximumimpact.com